A Crabtree Roots Book

TEACHER

DOUGLAS BENDER

People I Meet

CRABTREE
Publishing Company
www.crabtreebooks.com

School-to-Home Support for Caregivers and Teachers

This book helps children grow by letting them practice reading. Here are a few guiding questions to help the reader with building his or her comprehension skills. Possible answers appear here in red.

Before Reading:

- What do I think this book is about?
  - *This book is about teachers.*
  - *This book is about what a teacher does at work.*

- What do I want to learn about this topic?
  - *I want to learn where a teacher works.*
  - *I want to learn what a teacher does.*

During Reading:

- I wonder why...
  - *I wonder why some people become teachers.*
  - *I wonder why teachers use chalkboards.*

- What have I learned so far?
  - *I have learned that some teachers work in classrooms.*
  - *I have learned that teachers help people learn.*

After Reading:

- What details did I learn about this topic?
  - *I have learned that teachers can teach many different subjects.*
  - *I have learned that not all teachers teach in classrooms.*

- Read the book again and look for the vocabulary words.
  - *I see the word **classroom** on page 6, and the word **board** on page 8. The other vocabulary words are found on page 14.*

This is a **teacher**.

A teacher
helps people.

This teacher is in a **classroom**.

A teacher writes on
a **board**.

A teacher sits at a **desk**.

Do you know
a teacher?

Word List

Sight Words

a	is	this
at	on	you
do	people	
in	teacher	

Words to Know

board

classroom

desk

teacher

31 Words

This is a **teacher**.

A teacher helps people.

This teacher is in a **classroom**.

A teacher writes on a **board**.

A teacher sits at a **desk**.

Do you know a teacher?

People I Meet
TEACHER

Written by: Douglas Bender
Designed by: Rhea Wallace
Series Development: James Earley
Proofreader: Ellen Rodger
Educational Consultant: Christina Lemke M.Ed.

Photographs:
Shutterstock: ESB Professional: cover; michaeljung:
   p. 1, 3, 14; wavebreakmedia: p.5; Monkey Business
   Images: p. 7, 13, 14; Evgeniy Kalinovskiy: p.9, 14;
   Szasz-Fabian Illka Erikca: p. 10-11, 14

Library and Archives Canada Cataloguing in Publication

Title: Teacher / Douglas Bender.
Names: Bender, Douglas, 1992- author.
Description: Series statement: People I meet | "A Crabtree
   roots book".
Identifiers: Canadiana (print) 20210178566 |
   Canadiana (ebook) 20210178574 |
   ISBN 9781427141163 (hardcover) |
   ISBN 9781427141224 (softcover) |
   ISBN 9781427133427 (HTML) |
   ISBN 9781427134028 (EPUB) |
   ISBN 9781427141286 (read-along ebook)
Subjects: LCSH: Teachers—Juvenile literature.
Classification: LCC LB1775 .B46 2022 | DDC j371.1—dc23

Library of Congress Cataloging-in-Publication Data

Names: Bender, Douglas, 1992- author.
Title: Teacher / Douglas Bender.
Description: New York : Crabtree Publishing, 2022. |
   Series: People I meet - a Crabtree roots book | Includes index.
Identifiers: LCCN 2021014336 (print) | LCCN 2021014337 (ebook) |
   ISBN 9781427141163 (hardcover) |
   ISBN 9781427141224 (paperback) |
   ISBN 9781427133427 (ebook) |
   ISBN 9781427134028 (epub) |
   ISBN 9781427141286
Subjects: LCSH: Teachers--Juvenile literature.
Classification: LCC LB1775 .B436 2022 (print) |
   LCC LB1775 (ebook) | DDC 371.1--dc23
LC record available at https://lccn.loc.gov/2021014336
LC ebook record available at https://lccn.loc.gov/2021014337

Crabtree Publishing Company

www.crabtreebooks.com   1-800-387-7650

Printed in the U.S.A./062021/CG20210401

Published in the United States
Crabtree Publishing
347 Fifth Avenue, Suite 1402-145
New York, NY, 10016

Published in Canada
Crabtree Publishing
616 Welland Ave.
St. Catharines, Ontario L2M 5V6

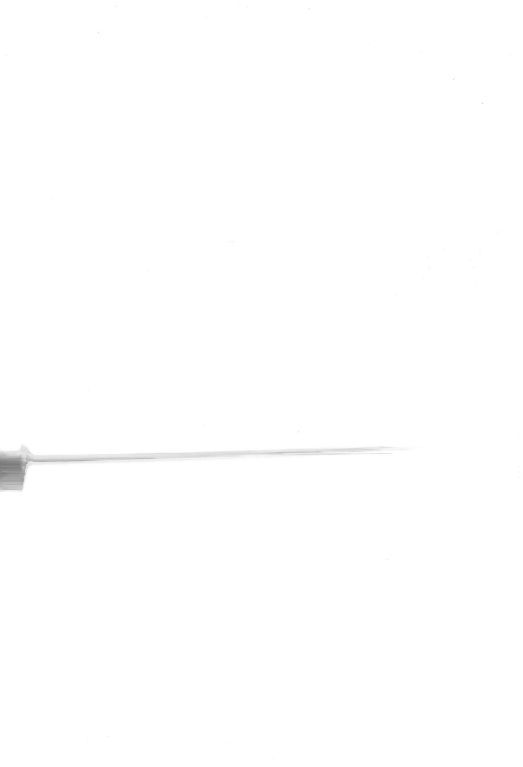